What's inside..

Saying these affirmations out loud will make you feel so powerful and ready for school.

#1 I am loved wherever I am

#2 I can question my worries

#3 I'm choosing to have an amazing day

#4 I have the power to enjoy school

#5 My confidence grows when I challenge myself

#6 I can ask for help

#7 My mistakes help me to learn and grow

#8 I am ready for any challenge

#9 I am doing my best

#10 I believe in me

#11 True friends will bring joy to my day

#12 Today I did my best, now my mind is set to rest

During the week families must go
separate ways,
school is your adventure,
a place for learning and play.

At first this might seem a scary
thing to do,
but you won't be alone,
you will have friends and teachers
too.

You are loved wherever you are and
whatever you do,
and you will always join paths again
when the day is through.

It can be helpful to write your worries down before school and turn them into helpful thoughts or resolve them with a grown up.

Worries are thoughts that are not helpful or kind,
and most don't come true they are just made up in your mind.

If you question your worries and work to send them away,
you can enjoy every part of your day.

"What if I get an answer wrong?"

↓

"Mistakes are a chance for me to learn!"

#3

"I'm choosing to have an amazing day"

There is always something to look forward to in your day.

It could be what you have for lunch, seeing your friends, a favourite lesson?

What do you look forward to at school?

Your thoughts and what you do in the morning can affect your whole day,
so try your best to think of school in a positive way.

Do things that make you feel good before you leave,
there is fun to be had and learning goals to achieve.

Your mind believes everything that you say, so keep telling it you are choosing to have an amazing day.

If there is something at school you
really don't want to do,
try your best not to think about it
until it's time to.

If you focus on not
wanting to do it all day,
that negative feeling won't go away.

Instead, choose not to think about what
the future might bring,
but work hard on enjoying the moment
you're in.

Practice being mindful with balloon
breathing.
As you breathe in, imagine your tummy
as a balloon getting bigger and bigger.
As you breathe out, the balloon slowly
deflates.

Confidence isn't about being loud
or not being scared when in front
of a crowd.

It is knowing you are amazing no
matter what people say,
no one can stop you from enjoying
your day.

It is not giving up when things are
going wrong,
by reminding yourself that you are
so brave and strong.

Repeat this 3 times:
"I am amazing just
the way I am"

If there is something at school you find hard or an answer you don't know, asking a teacher for help is how your brain will grow.

Asking an adult for help can make you feel better, sometimes problems can be solved by talking them through together.

Who can you ask for help?

Learning can be fun if you train your mind; to always cheer you on and be helpful and kind.

Turn around any unhelpful thoughts that you get,
instead of
saying I can't, just add the word yet.

Before giving up, try and find another way.
If you make a mistake, now you can learn. Hooray!

Is there anything you can't do YET but you are learning?

Learning something new takes time
and at first you will make mistakes,
but you are powerful and can do hard
things no matter how long it takes.

You may need to break things down
into steps that you can manage,
but if you put in the time and effort
you can take on any
challenge.

"This is too hard I give up!"

"This might take time and
effort..."

Don't worry about your friends work
or the scores from a test,
none of that matters if you did your
best.

Everyone is different there's no one
like you,
so where you are in learning
will be different too.

Stop comparing
yourself to
others.

You're the #1 you!

Talk to yourself like you would your
best friend
and you will feel love at school
from the start to the end.

Show yourself kindness when you are
finding things tough
and remind yourself that
your best is enough.

Imagine how you would talk to
someone you love if they were
having the same thoughts and
worries.
Talk to yourself this way!

During school there will be times for
you to play and having
a friend there could bring joy
to your day.

If you listen to others and always
choose to be kind,
a friend to play with should be
easy to find.

If you are feeling left out
or can't find something to do,
talk to a teacher
and they will try and help you.

When the school day is over try your best not to dwell,
on the parts of your day you feel didn't go so well.

Focus on the bits that made you feel good,
be proud of yourself for doing the best that you could.

You are loved no matter what happened today,
so let your mind rest,
it's time to relax and play.

If you ever feel sad about school or have
unhelpful thoughts,
you can read this book and remember
all that it taught.

You have the POWER to ENJOY SCHOOL.

Printed in Great Britain
by Amazon